Finesse Your Life

MW01320029

Finesse Your Life: Mind, Body and Spirit.

Copyright ©2017 Jennifer Slay. Printed in the United States of America.

Finesse Your Life and all references are a part of the Finesse Program of Jennifer Slay. All Rights Reserved.

No part of this book may be reproduced or transmitted in any form or by any means, electronically or mechanically, including photocopying, recording or by any information storage and retrieval system, without the expressed written consent from the author or publisher, except in cases of brief quotations embodied in critical articles and reviews.

For more information, contact Jennifer Slay at info@jenslay.com

Visit my website at: www.jenslay.com

Editor: Write On Communication Services
Illustrations: Lauren V | Brand Ya Flava
Book Cover Design: Lauren V | Brand Ya Flava

ISBN: 978-1548117085

Finesse Your Life:
Mind, Body, and Spirit

Jennifer Slay

Table of Contents

Acknowledgements 5

Introduction 6

Finesse Your Life - Mind 19

    Study 21

    Self Awareness 23

    Self Manage 27

    Kill the Inner Bully (I.B.) 31

    Alone Time & Sleep 33

    Good People 35

    Have a Goal. Enjoy the Journey. 37

    Be Mindful 39

    Count to 10 41

    Smile 42

Finesse Your Life – Body 55

    Acceptance 55

    Drink Water 60

    Personal Hygiene 63

    Undergarments 71

    Know Your Body Shape 73

    Know Your Undertone 77

    Exercise 79

    Sleep 83

    Good Posture 84

Finesse Your Life – Spirit 96
- Gratefulness 98
- Reflection 102
- Positive Affirmations 108
- Replenish 112
- Release 115
- Prayer & Meditation 118
- Family & Loved Ones 121
- Nature 123
- Get Sleep & Drink Water 126
- Laughter 128

About the Author 150

Acknowledgements

This book is dedicated to my sister, Sarah, who has always been an inspiration to my spirit, a shoulder to cry on, and the absolute best friend and sister any person could ever be blessed to have. Love you Baby Girl.

Introduction

"Be the change you want to see in the world." Gandhi.

Living life on purpose has become a catch phrase. It is a way of life that, if done right, will produce positive results for you, your loved ones and your community. Imagine it: doing what you love to do each and every day; living life by your own rules. Doesn't that sound amazing? It is an amazing feeling to set your schedule and live each day by your own design. However, most of us are hardwired to live within a prescribed formula. Many are taught to go to school, get good grades, graduate, go to post-secondary school, get a job, buy a house, get married, have children, work for 30 years, retire and THEN enjoy life. Does this describe your reality or the reality of someone you know? It describes the path that I was on.

To give you some context and a little peek into my life, my parents were both born in the Caribbean. My dad was born into a very proud but poor family. His way out was to follow the above formula and he did it well. Dad studied hard, went to one of the finest schools in the world – Oxford University in London, England. He became a teacher and followed the promotion trek, going on to become vice principal, then principal. His career culminated by becoming a university professor.

'When it ain't broke don't fix it,' was his thinking, so he and my mother drilled this formula into my sister and I from a young age. And you know what? It works! I lived it. I was the obedient child that did what I was told (for the most part). I grew up in a middleclass neighborhood and had a comfortable life. I went to school, got good grades, graduated, went to university, graduated, got a job, got married, bought a house, had some children, and began my work career of 30 years with intentions to retire in 2025. This was programmed into me. Forget that I had this burning desire to do other things, like sing, dance and speak at a professional level. Forget that I wanted to travel the world and see how people in other cultures live. Forget about wanting more for myself than what was prescribed to me. Obedience and fear held me captive. And you know what? I was miserable. First world problems, right? Wrong. Check it out. Whether you are born into a rich or poor family, you will not have peace in your heart or mind if you do not live by your own design and not as society or family expectations prescribe. *You will not find peace within you if you do not live life as you were destined to live it.*

My earlier life was a classic example of this. To make it worse, while living this prescribed life, I was always concentrating on the destination: just getting over *there*. I was concentrating so deeply that I was not enjoying the journey along the way. Actually, I did not even acknowledge the journey. This *journey* thing that many motivational speakers talk about is the real deal. When you focus on the end result without learning from the journey, without enjoying the journey, without accepting the journey - things can get messed up. At least, that was my experience. I had done what my parents prescribed – earned three degrees, got married, bought a house, had two cars in the driveway, had three children and was living the 'dream' but at the 17-year mark of the 30-year career journey I was miserable. Why? I did not enjoy or celebrate the successes that were made along the way. My husband and I lost ourselves in the getting-to-the-finish line part, so that we did not even recognize who we were when we finally lifted our heads up for air. It came to a point where we did things and made decisions that were out of character for both of us. Result: divorce, depression, self-doubt.

None of it seemed fair. I did everything the way I was told to do it (for the most part). So why wasn't I happy? Why did I always feel like something was missing? Why could I not find peace? Why was I always searching and not satisfied with what I had? Something inside was bothering me. The problem: the prescribed formula was not my path. And because it was not my path, my spirit could not be at peace. Solution: I had to figure some things out. I had to sit back and focus on my real issue. What did I really love to do? What filled my cup? What made me smile at the end of the day? What made me feel like I was a contributor to this world and not JUST taking up space?

When I sat to reflect and really think about these questions the answers were not that hard to come up with. I absolutely love to teach. I love to help. I love to share ideas. I love to speak. Once I determined my loves and passions, I had to determine why I was not doing these things; why I was following a different path. What was I afraid of? I was afraid of failing; I was afraid of venturing off on my own and creating my own "formula." I feared pursuing a life different than the one prescribed by my parents.

Like many folks, I was comfortable in my discomfort. I worked in a government job for 17years.This job came with full health benefits, job security, seniority, respect, a pay cheque every two weeks, and I was good at it. To pick up and leave this job - as a single mom to three boys - sounds crazy, right? I was also facing internal fears common to many, so I was trying to quell the voice of the inner bully throwing self-doubt into the mix. The voice seemed to be telling me I wasn't worth the risk that would lead to living life on purpose. I knew things had to change because I felt like I was drowning. I was dying inside and felt like I was taking up space by not living my life's purpose. This is when things started to change for me. Why am I telling you this? Because my story is not unique. So many of us have similar stories. I'm sharing my story because many will see their own struggles reflected in it or know someone else to whom it may be meaningful. You understand that there is something missing and you want to figure it out, right? And you will. I believe it. Question is, do you?

Taking control of your life does not mean that you call all of the shots. Let's be honest, sometimes things happen around us that are not in our control. A spouse decides to leave. Someone you love passes away. You do not get the promotion you want. Things happen. So what do you do? The only thing you can do is control your **reaction** to circumstances that happen around you. That phrase "I can't help it.

I just get so angry, and I lash out." Bull crap! You have control over yourself. You choose not to exercise it. Learning self-control will help you my friend - trust me. When you can control your reactions to things then you can help to create the space that surrounds you. Will negative things happen? Yes. Will you fall sometimes? Yes. Will it suck? Hell yes! However, I believe that the tips in this book will help you to be able to build up your resilience to face those hard times. The tips in this book will help you appreciate the good times too.

Nothing written in this book is brand new. Rather, I have compiled the most effective means to finesse your life by focusing on mind, body and spirit. Having worked in the human services field for nearly two decades, I have coached and counselled people through various issues, ranging from marital distress, to abuse issues, to just getting past the temporary pause that is often referred to as 'being stuck.' The following tips have helped many of the clients with whom I've worked to move forward. I have used much of this valuable information in my own journey. Please take what is useful to you to begin navigating the path that will finesse your life.

Most importantly, the way to start anything in this life is step up for yourself. Once you believe in you – the sky is the limit!

Secret Formula Time

To ensure that you are successful in implementing the tips to Finesse Your Life – Taking care of your Mind, Body, and Spirit you have to be willing to implement some changes. Can you commit to that? Can you commit to making changes in your life for the next 7, 14 or 21 days?

You may have heard that change is hard, but it really does not have to be. The reason change might be hard for you is because you are likely trying to change everything at once. For years, I wondered why New Year's resolutions never worked. Normally, around the end of December we often get nostalgic, then reflective about the year that's nearly over. We may decide that the year coming up is going to be 'our' year. All goals are going to be accomplished! Does this look familiar?

1. Exercise more
2. Spend more time with friends and family
3. Read more
4. Lose 20 pounds

5. Start my [insert project] that I've been wanting to do
6. Make more money

These goals seem doable right? Fairly realistic right? Tell the truth, do you have a list like this? Here is what typically happens with these goals. For the first week of January you are well on your way, and you are at the gym, on the phone with your friends, you got your books you want to read, you bought a new outfit that you want to fit into, you got the materials you need to start your project, and you have new ideas to make money. Week 2: still doing ok. Week 3: one goal has to be put aside for a minute. Week 4: another goal has to be put to the side but will get to it shortly. And by March, you don't even want to remember what your goals were because you feel so much guilt that you didn't carry through with what you said you were going to do. Why is this? And why do we put ourselves through this year after year?

There are a few problems with the above list. First, it's not specific enough. Second, you may have tried to implement the changes all at once without a real plan.

Want to know the secret to long lasting change? Change small, change often. It's like the secret of eating a whole elephant. Take one bite at a time, and eventually you will have consumed the elephant. (Just a note here – who really wants to consume an elephant? I know I'm being literal, but there isn't really a better subject to use in this metaphor.) In order to create lasting change in your life, focus on the change you want to make and do something towards that change daily until it becomes habitual. Then take on something else. Let me give you an example. Have you ever tried to lose weight? I have. Liquid shake diets seem to be a revolving fad. They work too – for a while. You suddenly are decreasing your intake of solid foods and taking in liquids. Logic says you will lose weight and you will. However, when you stop drinking the shakes and start eating solid foods again, you will put the weight back on – and maybe more. That happened to me and many others.

Every year, on January 1, many people start going to the gym religiously with the goal to lose weight. They go faithfully three times a week. Then twice weekly. Then once a week. Then they stop going altogether. **Here's the big secret** – *change small, change often.*

Losing weight means you must make some lifestyle changes. Here's what worked for me: I stopped eating after 7 p.m. Within a week I lost five pounds without going to the gym. Those who increase their intake of water and decrease the amount of sugary drinks consumed will start to see the changes in their body shape within a week or two. These two very small changes are easy to implement, and they have been proven to be effective. Once you implement them, you will feel like you already have a win. Small changes + consistency = effective results. If you want to add going to the gym – go for it. But if you are a person who never goes to the gym then maybe a good goal is to plan to work out once or twice a week and do that consistently for three weeks. Then increase the amount of times you go if that's what you choose to do. *Change small, change often*. It may take a while. I did not say that change was fast. However, when you change small and change often it will last.

Since you are reading this book, I'm making the assumption that you want to make changes to better your life – mind, body and spirit. Essentially, you want to Finesse your Life to create your space. My suggestion is that you read through the 10 ways to effectively create change in each of the areas and then pick two to start. Two from the Mind section, two from the Body section and two from the Spirit section. Work on those for a couple of weeks.

Journal your progress. In order to see where you are, you have to know where you've been. So get a journal and document how you feel and what your goals are now. Document at least one success each day and write down something you could have done better. If the only success you had was that you woke up and got out of bed – celebrate that. Nothing is too small to be celebrated. BUT don't settle for that. Complacency is not the goal. Striving to better yourself so you are the best version of you – that's the goal. To make it easier, after each section of this book is an area for making notes and questions to help you get moving and on your way.

Sometimes support is needed to create the goals you need to move forward and plan steps to make those goals a reality. Congratulations, you've come to the right place. Find Jen's Top 10 Tips for Goal Setting on my YouTube channel and the ebook on my website. It will be a really quick read. Or, contact me at info@jenslay.com and together we can figure out your next steps. I'm here to serve you. My goal in life is to help as many people as possible realize their full potential. My purpose is to help you see/rediscover your greatness within and then help you share that greatness with the world.

You are in charge of your life. This is true despite what you are doing right now, despite your current circumstances and despite who signs your pay cheque, YOU are in charge of your life. YOU make the choices and decisions that are going to create your reality. You may not like the choices you have in front of you, but if you are stuck, start with making small consistent changes that will give you new strength mentally, emotionally and physically. Implement the tips in this book in your life. Then, get a coach. Whether it is me or another certified coach, getting the right coach is essential. A coach will kick your butt and cheer you on. S/he is a neutral party who sees things objectively to help you get clarity and focus on what you need to do next. A coach will keep you accountable. Remember this, the only person stopping you from being the success you want to be or that you could be - is you. If the universe puts something in your heart, no one can stop it from coming to fruition – except you.

You are amazing and as one of the greatest speakers in the world has said (Les Brown) – you have greatness within you. I believe that. Do you?

Read and enjoy the following tips. At the end of each section, you will find an area where you can jot notes and create your plan. Be deliberate in your plan and your goal will come to fruition. I hope our paths meet and we can enjoy part of the journey of life together.

Believe in you,

Jen

Finesse Your Life - Mind

"Change your thinking, change your life." - Ernest Holmes

The most powerful thing God gave us was our mind. Look at what human beings have accomplished with the power of the mind in just the last 100 years. I just look at what's been accomplished during my own lifetime – the home computer is now in nearly every household, whereas when I was a young child – who knew what a computer was? The only people who had cell phones when I was young were doctors and they looked nothing like the way they do now. They were initially as big and bulky as a shoe box. Or athletics – we have human beings running at speeds of nine seconds per 100 metres. Records are being broken every day. The power of the mind is beyond what any of us can fathom. So what is the difference between those who achieve great things by using the power of their minds and those who do not?

Is it resources?

Is it intelligence?

Is it work ethic?

No. It is none of these.

A book entitled Emotional Intelligence 2.0 states:

> "Not education. Not experience. Not knowledge or intellectual horsepower. None of these serve as an adequate predictor as to why one person succeeds and another doesn't There is something else going on that society doesn't seem to account for...We observe supposedly brilliant and well-educated people struggle, while others with few obvious skills or attributes flourish. And we ask ourselves why?"[1]

The authors of Emotional Intelligence 2.0, argue that Emotional Intelligence is what differentiates the successful from the not so successful. The ability to be self-aware, the ability to self-manage, the ability to be socially aware and the ability to manage relationships successfully is what makes a person or at least creates an atmosphere for a person to be successful. However, before any of that, I would argue that success in life starts with

---

[1] Bradberry, T. and Greeves, J. (2009) *Emotional Intelligence 2.0.* TalentSmart: United States

belief of possibility. The possibility of believing in something that you have not yet done. This belief in self is then followed by a plan and action steps to accomplish that plan. Once you have this belief – the starting point – you then must become a student of yourself. You must know yourself and how you tick. That is the secret formula of where the power lies. We are emotional creatures and we react emotionally to things that happen to us BUT to harness the ability to control thoughts and actions that follow an initial emotional reaction – THAT separates you from the average person. The ability to do this is to become AWARE. The next 10 tips are going to help you to hone in on your ability to be more aware of yourself and those around you. By implementing these steps, you will learn to *Finesse your Mind*.

Study

Study – always acquire knowledge. The acquisition of knowledge is something that should never stop. Think of the mind like a machine or I often compare the mind to a computer. It remembers and stores everything. And it will sort everything. What you put into your mind is exactly what is going to come out. If you fill your mind with garbage then garbage is going to come out. If you feed it with junk, then junk will be what it produces. However, if you put good in – good will come out.

Surround yourself with positive people who are smarter than you - people you can learn from. These people will make you strive to be a better version of yourself.

Make it a goal to read daily (at the very least weekly), as it allows your brain to feed and to gain more knowledge. With more knowledge comes the ability to think more creatively and to think about different ideas. Maybe even produce new ideas. Acquiring knowledge helps you to ask questions and not just accept what is told to you. Acquiring knowledge helps you to be able to come up with solutions to problems or improve upon solutions that are already out there. Think of the airplane, the lightbulb, the traffic light, think of the computer. All of these things had to come from an idea. All of these things required study and an ability to think creatively and intuitively.

Many people will say to me, "I wish I had time to read." Well, you do. We all do. We just have to make it a priority. Think outside of the box. Not everyone enjoys reading and getting lost in a book. They may be more auditory learners. There are so many audio books available now. It does not take much to go onto YouTube, type in the name of a book and then listen to it. Take at least 30 minutes during your day to listen to or read a book. With technology as it is today, we can record our favourite shows and binge watch them later. Take the 30 minutes that you would be watching a television show (which is watching other people work, by the way) and use that 30 minutes to feed your mind. Your mind craves knowledge – feed it. Here are a few ideas that will help you with this tip.

> ➢ Schedule reading/listening time into your calendar. You are more likely to accomplish your goal if you write it down. You will do what you prioritize, so schedule in your time.
> ➢ Depending on when you are most creative, go to bed 30 minutes earlier and wake up 30 minutes earlier, so that you can have time to read/listen.
> ➢ Take stock of areas of your life where you want to improve and find books about that area – then read them.

Self Awareness

Self-awareness – become the best student of you. A book referenced earlier, Emotional Intelligence 2.0, takes a look at what makes a successful person truly successful. Many automatically think that if you have a high IQ then you will be able to succeed in life. There should be no issue right? Wrong. Your IQ actually does not play a significant role in your level of success. However your EQ - Emotional Intelligence - plays a vital role in your ability to succeed.

Many of us spend a lot of time studying other people, studying various topics/issues or taking care of others. We spend so much time doing this that we forget that we have to know and take care of ourselves first. "But Jen, that's being selfish. We can't put ourselves first!" My response: yes you can and you should. Have you ever flown in an airplane before? Prior to take off, the flight attendant talks to the passengers about what to do in an emergency: if the oxygen levels drop or if an emergency landing is needed the first thing you do is to put the oxygen mask on **yourself** so that you can then help someone else. What is the point of passing out while putting the mask on someone else first? Who benefits from that? Take care of yourself.

In addition to that, you must also be aware of yourself. Study yourself. Understand the good and the not so good. Let's not fool ourselves into thinking we don't have areas of our lives we can improve upon and let's not forget or minimize the areas of our lives where we do very well. As mentioned at the beginning of this section – self-awareness is understanding yourself. It is becoming clear on what you do well, what motivates you and what upsets you (For help fully understanding this, reference Emotional Intelligence 2.0).

Ultimately being self-aware is being aware of what makes you tick, understanding your emotions. This allows you to control them and not let emotions control you.

Knowing what will push your buttons and how to manage having your buttons pushed is being self-aware. How can you become more self-aware? Here are some suggestions to get you on your way:

> Take stock of yourself several times a day. Take a moment and think about what you are feeling throughout the day. Do it purposefully. Do it especially when you are feeling really good and when you may be feeling really low. Try to figure out very specifically what you are feeling and why you are feeling it. What precipitated that feeling?

Understand who and what pushed your buttons, so that you can develop your own game plan to best manage those emotions next time they creep up. Make sure you enter this information in the journal that was mentioned earlier.
- ➢ Take responsibility. We all react to situations. Again, the goal here is to control those reactions. Play the story out to the end. How is your reaction going to impact those around you? This should not determine what your reaction will be; however, it should inform you as to what your reaction could be.
- ➢ Feel what you need to feel and be grateful for it. If you are feeling low – feel low but don't stay there. Just as if you are feeling great, feel great, but at some point you have to level off so that you are just ok. Finding your balance or equilibrium is important for you to maintain emotional balance. Note: we tend to want to avoid negative feelings. We do not want to hurt, so we will busy ourselves with projects, or with events or with work so we do not feel the hurt. But feeling the hurt is the fastest way to get through it and move on with

your life. Avoidance will only be a delay to what you will eventually have to feel and deal with.

Self Manage

Self-manage – control your emotions. Flying off the handle and losing your cool does nothing for you but create stress and anxiety for you and everyone around you. In order to effectively manage your emotions, you must be aware of them, so self-awareness and self-management go hand in hand.

How do you handle yourself when confronted with a difficult situation? Do you explode? Or do you breathe deep? Start thinking of solutions and stop focusing on the problem. How do you handle yourself when great things happen to you? Do you move forward impulsively or do you reflect and consider, then move forward to ensure you are doing what is best for you and for others impacted as well?

You may be a person who never gets openly upset and you may have a great poker face so you may figure that you do not have to think about this area – you are wrong. We all have to become experts in managing ourselves whether we are faced with a positive thing or a negative thing. For example, when you come into unexpected money – does it blow through your fingers like the wind, or do you sit and plan out what your next best move will be? Managing yourself through the good and the not so good are equally important.

Many of the tools to best self-manage are listed below in more depth but here are a few techniques to help:

> Breathe – it is important to be breathing correctly in order to think optimally. Do you notice that when you are anxious or frightened you will take very shallow breaths? Notice that when you do this you cannot think clearly and you become flustered? If you take a look at how you breathe regularly, you are likely breathing in a very similar fashion as to what I just described above. Correct breathing is when you completely fill your lungs with hair (tummy out when air goes in and sucked in when air goes out). According to Bradbury & Greaves (2009), the reason it is so important to breath correctly is because your brain requires 20 per cent of your total oxygen intake. Your lungs are created to take in the exact amount of air that you need. The brain controls your thinking and

managing your mood so when you are not taking in sufficient oxygen you will experience mood swings and poor concentration. Throughout the day focus on taking slow, deep breaths.
- ➢ Visualization – one of my mentors, Lisa Nichols, has had so many tele-classes on the power of visualization. You may have heard Oprah talk about it, as well as many successful people in business. Visualize what it is you want, then act as though you have it.

I've read that the brain has a difficult time distinguishing between what you see with your eyes and what you visualize in your mind. Apparently, MRI scans of people's brains taken while they are watching the sun set are no different than scans taken when the same people visualize a sunset in their mind. The same brain regions are active in both scenarios. Isn't that something?

It is suggested that you visualize your reactions and management of your behaviour to what you want to actually have happen. Visualize it to the point that you can feel the feelings, and see yourself in the midst of the situation. Focus on the details – what do you see, hear and feel?

This visualization will help your brain to create the neuropathways that will develop the habits you want to form in managing stressful (good and bad) situations.

Here are some suggestions to get you started:
- Find a mentor. Who do you admire for his or her coolness under pressure? Once you find this person, mimic his or her behaviors. Be you, but adopt your mentor's characteristics that you admire. Successful people copy success. Why reinvent the wheel when you really don't have to?
- Take care of yourself. Eat well and drink water. Taking care of your body is vitally important to success. Ensuring you are feeding your body properly is very important. Think of your body as a top performing vehicle. It needs a particular type of oil and gas to work at its peak performance – just like you. If you are constantly driving your vehicle without proper maintenance it's going to break down – just as you will. Our bodies were made to work, to create, to dream, to be active, but they need to be fueled to work optimally. The consequence of not feeding your body

is far worse than taking the time to take care of yourself. The human brain is 75 per cent water, so drinking sufficient quantities of water to fuel your most important organ is vital to clear thinking and good judgment.

Kill the Inner Bully (I.B.)

Kill the I.B. with kindness. Most of us have an inner bully (I.B). That inner voice that tells us we cannot do something. It will take effort to quiet the I.B. but doing so is imperative to having a clear mind. Really pay attention to the messages that you are telling yourself – good, bad, and neutral. If you have a thought or an idea that you want to try - go with it. Your gut reaction is usually the right one. It is when we sit and think about situations too long that we talk ourselves out of it. This tip is going to take practice and will develop over time. Unless you were fortunate enough to grow up in an environment in which you were encouraged to take risks, forge your own path and think positively, it is easier to believe you cannot do something than it is to believe you can. Remember, if you do not believe in yourself, why should anyone else take the time to believe in you?

So how do you quiet the inner bully? It will take repeated action to control this negative voice.

> Daily affirmations are crucial to killing your I.B. with kindness. A great time to practice this skill is when you are in front of the mirror. Write a mantra and recite it to yourself daily. A mantra that I took from a movie and that I had my kids repeat everyday was "I am smart. I am kind. I am important." Tell yourself who you are, even if you don't quite believe it yet. You have a purpose – own it.

Dr. Carmen Harra, from the Huffington Post, wrote: Affirmations help purify our thoughts and restructure the dynamic of our brains so that we truly begin to think nothing is impossible. The word affirmation comes from the Latin *affirmare*, originally meaning "to make steady, strengthen."[2]

---

[2] Harra, C. (2017, March 13). 21 Mantras that will change your life. *Huffington Post*. Retrieved from:
http://www.huffingtonpost.com/entry/21-mantras-that-will-change-your-life_us_58c4e8a3e4b0c3276fb785e5

Strengthening your belief in yourself and silencing the inner bully is vital to your ability to finesse your mind.

Alone Time & Sleep

Alone time and sleep – Although we are social creatures, we need time to rejuvenate. Think of yourself like a cell phone: when a cell phone is fully charged it works optimally. When the battery is low, the phone does not work as well; it works but certain apps won't come up. It works, but the phone runs slower. This is like your brain – it will work no matter how hard you work your body but for it to work optimally, it needs rest and to be recharged. Sleep is essential to staying sharp.

Lack of sleep impairs cognitive ability. When you do not get enough sleep you may become irritable, moody and lack good judgement. Further, lack of sleep can affect memory, ability to multitask and flatten emotional responses. Sleep is essential to health and wellbeing. While you sleep, your body is at rest and this is where the most healing happens, The National Heart, Lung and Blood Institute has reported that

> Sleep plays a vital role in good health and well-being throughout your life.

> Getting enough quality sleep at the right times can help protect your mental health, physical health, quality of life, and safety.[3]

The way you feel while you're awake depends in part on what happens while you're sleeping. During sleep, your body is working to support healthy brain function and maintain your physical health. In children and teens, sleep also helps support growth and development.

The damage from sleep deficiency can occur in an instant (such as a car crash), or it can harm you over time. For example, ongoing sleep deficiency can raise your risk for some chronic health problems. It also can affect how well you think, react, work, learn, and get along with others.

Listen to your body when it is saying it is tired. You will be more productive if you are rested than when you are running on empty.

A few tips to encourage good sleep:

- Turn off all screens at least an hour before you go to sleep. The blue light that comes from screens can impact

---

[3] *U.S. National Lung, Heart and Blood Institute* (2017). Retrieved from: https://www.nhlbi.nih.gov/

our production of the hormone melatonin. Our bodies need melatonin as it helps control our sleep and wake cycles. Insufficient production of this hormone can negatively impact our sleep. Turn off the screens!
- Exercise regularly. Studies show that exercising (especially vigorous exercise) will help encourage good sleep.
- Practice a relaxing bed time routine. Human beings are creatures of habit. If we practice a relaxing routine prior to bed, it will become like a signal to our brains that it is time to go to sleep and your body will respond accordingly.

Good People
Listen to and surround yourself with good people. Our minds are powerful. They are the most powerful computers ever invented. When a computer constantly visits sites with viruses and spam, it slows it down. The computer is not able to get you to where you need to go right away; it gets jammed up. It takes more time to clean out and recharge. Our minds are the same. When we spend our time with people who gossip, who are negative or who constantly put us down, it depletes our energy and slows us down. When we constantly watch

violence and tragedy on television, it hurts our spirits. Be mindful of what you feed your mind. Listen to positive speakers, watch positive programs and surround yourself with positive people. You may think the negativity rolls off your back, but it gets into your subconscious mind and impacts your behavior inwardly and outwardly.

Suggestions:

> Do not watch the news right before bed or when you first awake. When you wake up your mind is very aware (even though you feel groggy) of what is going on and is most receptive to ideas. It is for this reason researchers say to do daily affirmations or listen to something positive as soon as you wake up.

Before you sleep, your subconscious mind will ruminate on what you last think about. This, too, is a good time to do daily affirmations or listen to something positive.

> Keep negative people at arm's length. Be very protective of your inner circle. This does not mean to surround yourself with "yes" people. Yes people are people that will always say yes to

you even if they know what you want to do is not a good idea. Genuine, caring people are going to love you and care for you enough to let you know that what you are doing is going to hurt you. It is not easy to remove people from your life, but it is a necessity in taking the next step to a better you.

Have a Goal. Enjoy the Journey.

Have a goal and enjoy the journey. One of the most important tips to finessing one's mind is to have goals to work toward and look forward to. When you know what your end result will be it is easier to enjoy the journey. BUT do not be like I was. Do not only focus on the end result and bypass the victories along the way. When difficult times threaten to stop you right in your tracks embrace them. This seems counter intuitive but look at the opportunity for growth in that difficulty. Let's look at a plant. When a seed is planted in the ground, the goal for that seed is to break through the earth to get to sunlight. However, before it can get to the sunlight it has to go through a period of growth and push through the earth, endure the weather and ward off bugs. So what does the plant do? It develops a toughness so that harsh weather cannot blow it away. It develops defensive colours or thorns to deter bugs and other threats. Bottom line: they adapt. When you know where you're going and what's waiting for you at the finish line, the difficult times are easier to endure, the lessons are easier to learn, so you adapt. There is much more appreciation and love for the end result when you can enjoy your journey.

Suggestions:
- How do you set a goal? First, ensure that the goal is one that will motivate you. If your goal is to make more money, write that down. Once you have your goal down, ask yourself why you want to achieve that goal. It is your why that is going to do the motivating. If you want to make more money because you want to feed your family, that's a pretty strong why. Your why has to be important to you and mean something to you. So in setting the goal, ensure you incorporate your why.
- Believe you can achieve it. Belief can make all the difference in whether or not you accomplish your goal. Believing in yourself is important. One way to get that belief is to hear it, so repeat it over and over and over again. Post your goal on your mirror, in your journal, on your fridge – all of the places that you

will see it. When you see it repeat it. And do this over and over again. Our minds are powerful. The simple act of seeing, hearing, and believing can make a world of difference in the journey from where you are now to where you will be a year from now.
- ➢ Make the goal SMART: Specific, Measurable, Achievable, Realistic, Timely.
- ➢ Find an accountability partner. Someone who is not afraid to be truthful with you during the hard times. Make your action plan and stick with it.

Believe that you can achieve whatever it is you put your mind to. You MUST believe that. Before the automobile, no one thought that people could get from point A to point B in a box on wheels without a horse. Before the first airplane, no one thought it was possible to get from point A to point B in a tube with wings. Before there was electricity, no one thought there could be light without fire. Notice something here? "No one thought..." but because one person believed...you finish the sentence.

Be Mindful

Be mindful of what is going into your brain. As the saying goes – what goes in, must come out.

I absolutely love R&B music and pop music. I love the beat, the rhythms, and the melody lines. I was not a person who would pay attention to the lyrics. Music was part of my daily life: I would sing the songs and listen to songs in the car, in the evenings, at gatherings – you get what I'm saying. For some reason, there was a period of time where I was no longer listening to music as much. It might have been when my four year old started singing the lyrics to R. Kelly's You Remind Me of My Jeep song "You remind me of my jeep – I want to ride it. Something like my sound – I want to pump it". Something wrong with that picture. But that's when I started to really pay attention to what I was listening to. I started to pay attention to the lyrics and the words that I would sing and put out there. They were all about heartbreak and turmoil. Rarely were there uplifting songs that spoke life into my life. So I started to pay attention to EVERYTHING I would listen to. Anything that was negative I cut out. You know what happened? My mood lifted. I was more hopeful. I was more positive. I stopped listening to the news first thing when I woke up. I started listening to motivational tapes or motivational music. Everything in my life started to turn around. This is a simple test

— try it. It's amazing how one small change can create such a huge impact in one's life.

Suggestions:

> ➢ Take stock of what you are listening to and cut out the negative music, programs, and, as mentioned above, people.
> ➢ Purposefully listen to one positive thing per day, whether that is a motivational speaker, audio book or music.

Count to 10

Take your time and count to 10. If you have to, count to 10 again. And repeat counting to 10 until you are at a place where you can move forward. So often we put ourselves on the time clocks of other people. But sometimes, you just have to take 10 to gather your thoughts and move forward with a clear mind.

Bradbury & Greeves (2009) wrote it best:

> "When you feel yourself getting frustrated or angry, stop yourself by taking in a deep breath and saying the number one to yourself as you exhale. Keep breathing and counting until you reach the number 10. The counting and breathing will relax you and stop you from taking rash action long enough to

regain your composure and develop a more clear, rational perspective of the situation".

An immediate reaction to things is fueled by the emotional part of our brains. Taking a bit of time and breathing will give you time to dip into the rational part of the brain which will allow you to be in control of yourself and thus how you react.

Suggestions:
- Count to 10. In reality, if you are in the middle of a business meeting and you take a time out to count to 10, you may get some rather interesting looks from your peers, but the point of this exercise is to get you to just take a time out. Whether it is to the count of 10 or the count of five, just take a moment and chill.
- Breathe deeply and slowly when you feel yourself getting anxious or upset. This will force your body to calm down and help release any anxiety so that you can think more clearly.

Smile

Smile at yourself. This is one of my favorites because it seems just so silly. I love to be silly and I love to laugh. Think about this: when you walk down the street and someone smiles at you, your natural reaction is to smile back right? Even if it's just to be nice, you will smile back. This works internally as well: if you look in a mirror and smile at yourself, believe it or not, you will genuinely smile back. Sounds crazy but think about this. If you are sitting and smiling (even if it is forced) at yourself in the mirror, you are going to start smiling (genuinely) back. Believe it or not, there is science to back this up. According to Jennifer Smith of Lifehack.org, "Neurotransmitters called endorphins are released when you **smile**. These are triggered by the movements of the muscles in your face, which is interpreted by your **brain**, which in turn releases these chemicals. Endorphins are responsible for making us feel happy, and they also help lower stress levels."[4]

Furnham of Psychology Today writes[5]:

Each time you smile you throw a little feel-good party in your brain. The act of smiling activates neural messaging that benefits your health and happiness.

---

[4] Smith, J. (2017) 7 Benefits of Smiling and Laughing that you didn't know about. *Life Hack*. Retrieved from:
http://www.lifehack.org/articles/communication/7-benefits-smiling-and-laughing.html

[5] Furnham, A. (2014, October 31). The surprising psychology of smiling. *Psychology Today*. Retrieved from:
https://www.psychologytoday.com/blog/sideways-view/201410/the-surprising-psychology-smiling

For starters, smiling activates the release of neuropeptides that work toward fighting off stress. Neuropeptides are tiny molecules that allow neurons to communicate. They facilitate messaging to the whole body when we are happy, sad, angry, depressed, and excited. The feel good neurotransmitters dopamine, endorphins and serotonin are all released when a smile flashes across your face as well. This not only relaxes your body, but it can lower your heart rate and blood pressure.

The endorphins also act as a natural pain reliever – 100 per cent organically and without the potential negative side effects of synthetic concoctions.

Finally, the serotonin release brought on by your smile serves as an anti-depressant/mood lifter. Many of today's pharmaceutical anti-depressants also influence the levels of serotonin in your brain, but with a smile, you again don't have to worry about negative side effects – and you don't need a prescription from your doctor.

Smiling, forced or not has a positive effect on your mood, decreases stress levels and can make those around you feel better[6]. Essentially, smiling is good for your mind.

RECAP:

Ten tips:

1. Study
2. Become Self Aware
3. Learn to Self-Manage
4. Kill the Inner Bully with Kindness
5. Alone Time and Sleep
6. Listen and Surround yourself with Positive People
7. Have a goal and enjoy the journey
8. Be mindful of what is going in
9. Take Your Time
10. Smile

Which two can you start with?

_____
_____
_____
_____

I believe in changing small and changing often to create lasting change. I will be accountable to myself and to [insert your

---

[6] Widrich, R. (2016, April 1). The science of smiling: A guide to the most powerful gesture. *Buffer Social*. Retrieved from:
https://blog.bufferapp.com/the-science-of-smiling-a-guide-to-humans-most-powerful-gesture

coach/accountability partner's name]
_____
__ with regards to my commitment to Finesse my Life – Mind.

For each goal I will write down HOW I will implement the goal, WHEN I will implement the goal, WHAT my expectation and desired outcome is for the goal, and WHY this goal is important to me.

Remember, change small change often. Start with two and add as time goes on.

Starting on [insert date] _____ I will implement these two goals.

1._____
_____
_____
_____
_____
_____
_____
_____
_____
_____
_____

_____
_____
_____
_____
_____
_____
_____
_____

Record your success daily.

2._____
_____
_____
_____
_____
_____
_____
_____
_____
_____
_____
_____
_____
_____
_____
_____

_____

_____

Record your success daily.

As I begin to achieve my goals I will implement the other tips to add to my success!

3.

_____

_____

Record your success daily.

4.

_____
_____
_____
_____
_____
_____
_____
_____
_____
_____
_____
_____
_____
_____
_____

_____

Record your success daily.

5.

_____

Record your success daily.

6.

_____
_____
_____
_____
_____
_____
_____
_____
_____
_____
_____
_____
_____
_____
_____
_____

_____

Record your success daily.

7.

_____
_____
_____
_____
_____
_____

Record your success daily.

8.

Finesse Your Life – Mind, Body, and Spirit

_____
_____
_____
_____
_____
_____

_____

Record your success daily.

9.

_____
_____
_____
_____
_____
_____
_____
_____
_____
_____
_____
_____
_____
_____
_____

Record your success daily.

10.

Record your success daily.

Finesse Your Life – Body

Movement is a medicine for creating change in a person's physical, emotional and mental states. Carol Welch

Your physical health is vital to how you enjoy your life. Have you heard that saying "Life is short" or "Time is just flying by"? Guess what? Life may be short but it is the longest thing that you or I will ever do. Take control of your physical health. You have one life – how do you choose to live it? Here are my top 10 tips to Finesse Your Life - Body.

Acceptance
Accept who you are, what you look like, and how you got to where you are. But keep in mind that acceptance does not mean complacency. Often when you hear anything to do with the word "body" your mind goes to weight. There is such an obsession with weight and body image that it is almost an epidemic.

According to Kay Uzoma of Livingstrong.com, Americans are dieting by the millions. "The Boston Medical Center indicates that approximately 45 million Americans diet each year and spend $33 billion on weight-loss products in their pursuit of a trimmer, fitter body."[7]

In Britain, according to Poulter of DailyMail UK, there were over 29 million British people who attempted to lose weight last year.[8]

According to the Canadian Women's Network, in Canada today, between 80 and 90 per cent of women and girls are unhappy with the way they look.[9]

There are many theories as to why so many people, especially women, are unhappy about their physical appearance, but one of the most important keys to Finessing Your Body and loving your life is to first **accept what you look like**. You are who you are. Once you have accepted yourself and your body for what it is, then make the decision to improve on it if you

---

[7] Uzoma, K. (2015). Percentage of people who diet every year. *Livestrong*. Retrieved from: http://www.livestrong.com/article/308667-percentage-of-americans-who-diet-every-year/

[8] Poulter, S. (2014, January 2). A record two in three women have dieted in past year, while 44% of men were among the 29 million Britons trying to slim. *DailyMail UK*.
http://www.dailymail.co.uk/femail/article-2532602/More-half-UK-tried-lose-weight-2013-95-women-STILL-worry-theirs-staggering-statistics-reveal.html

[9] Canadian Women's Health Network (2012). *Body Image and the Media*. Retrieved from: http://www.cwhn.ca/node/40776

want to. The goal is to be healthy – NOT SKINNY.

I went to the Caribbean one summer for a funeral. The women in the Caribbean are diverse – beautifully diverse. Light skinned mocha brown, to dark skinned glistening chocolate – the women there are every shade of brown. However, my cousin informed me that many women were not happy with their complexions. They wanted to be light skinned and therefore bleaching had become extremely popular. Bleaching means exactly that: people purchase a product that they use or consume to make their skin complexion lighter. In many cultures and countries this is not uncommon. From the Far East to the tip of South America to the northern tip of North America, for hundreds of years skin colour has said something about your status: the lighter, the better. This is a sad sort of affairs, but the Western influence has been and is strong. In fact, sales in the global market for skin lighteners is projected to reach nearly $19.8 billion US by 2018! This is so odd to me; we are not ever satisfied with what we have!

As darker skinned persons of the world try to lighten their skin, the lighter skinned persons of the world try to darken their skin through tanning in the sun or artificially in a tanning bed. Not being content with being who you are is issue number one cause of mental anguish. Many companies are realizing their social responsibility and jumping on board by making efforts to show images of real women of varying complexions and sizes to help the growing discontentment of young girls and women. My thought? When deciding if you should change your appearance, ask yourself this basic question:

> ➢ Am I healthy?

If the answer is yes leave it at yes. Do not include: "Yes, I'm healthy BUT I'd like a rounder butt" or "I'd like bigger breasts," or "I'd like…" Accept who you are and what you look like. This does not mean that you can't work towards a goal of achieving a rounder butt, bigger breasts, or whatever else it is that you want, but it does mean loving yourself for who you are. I would love to have bigger breasts. When God was giving them out I must have been napping, but when I was in sports having small breasts was an advantage to me. I did not have back problems like many of my bigger breasted friends. If I want to have more cleavage, I just need to wear a padded bra. Not a big deal. I'm the queen of finding the positive in any situation and you can do the same.

When I was a teenager in the 90s, being shapely was just coming into style with the help of more natural looking models like Cyndi Crawford, Linda Evangelista and Claudia Schaffer. Although all tall and thin, they were not bone thin. Being born to Caribbean parents and having a mother who could cook the top chef out of the kitchen any day of the week, I had a love affair with food. To deny myself enjoyment of her cooking because I wanted to be really thin didn't make sense to me. Full disclosure: I was naturally tall and thin for my age BUT I had shape. I had a butt, a big butt. I had a big butt when it was not in style to have a big butt. My big butt was not going to go anywhere. I did not have YouTube to run to in order to find out how to slim down a big butt and, frankly, I didn't want to. I embraced my big butt and many others wanted to as well– lol. I had a choice: either learn to wear clothing that complemented my shape or worry about this butt I inherited from my parents. I chose the former. This is a choice that I hope you will also make. Once you accept what your body looks like that's when the fun begins.

If you are unhealthy and need to make some lifestyle changes, see a medical professional and start a healthy meal plan. But there is no reason why you shouldn't embrace your fierceness until you're at an ideal weight. Follow these nine other tips and you will exude the confidence that is already there but may be masked by your insecurities.

Drink Water

Drink Water – This seems so very basic but so many of us do not drink nearly enough water. Our bodies need water to survive. Water consumption helps us have healthy hair, nails, skin and internal organs. Most importantly, it helps our brains. Every cell in our bodies requires water to function properly because our bodies are composed of up to 60 per cent water.

There are two reasons here for why you should drink more water

- ➢ Physical wellbeing for the external body
- ➢ Physical wellbeing for the internal body

I know without a shadow of a doubt when I have not been drinking enough water. Have you ever experienced what I'm about to share? So at times my lips will get chapped. And I am a picker. I pick. So I start to peel the dead skin away on my lip – attractive – I know. But if you have ever had a chapped lip then you know that when you peel one part, then you have to peel another and eventually after all the peeling there is bleeding and it's just a mess right? Having chapped lips is a clear indicator that I am dehydrated.

Take a look at your nails. Are they cracked and brittle? Do they break easy? Again, it is from lack of water.

Do you have dry, ashy skin? Again, a lack of moisture. Here is why.

We primarily lose water through breathing, urination, and sweating. So we have to replenish that water loss in order to function at our optimal level. Please keep in mind I did not say replenish with any kind of liquid drink, like pop/soda or juice. You must consume WATER. If you don't like the taste of water there are some flavored products that you can drop into water to make it taste better, but those are often chemically based so using cucumber, lime, lemon or orange slices to flavour your water is preferred. You will drink what you enjoy. However, this one tip will help to change your life. I know it sounds dramatic but it just shows how important this point is. Check out this example.

Take a look at a plant that has not been watered. The leaves droop and look wilted and some of the leaves turn brown. Once you give that plant some water - within a minute –the plant perks up; the stem is stronger, and the leaves lift and the plant stretches towards the light. The human body is similar. Without enough water our eyes look sunken; our thoughts are not clear; skin is dry; hair is wiry, and lips are chapped. If you drink eight glasses of 250 ounces of water per day, within 24 hours you will see and feel the difference. Hands, feet, and lips – the extremities – are the first to be visibly seen as lacking water. Once you start drinking enough they will feel and look better because you are hydrated. Your thought processes will be clearer. Your body functions i.e. digestion will be better. You will have more energy. Your body will be better equipped to get rid of toxins. Water is essential to improved health.

It would be so easy to just tell you do something and move on, but I know that change is not always easy and providing some practical means to accomplish this goal can really help so I'm going to show you how easy it is to get your eight glasses in per day

> Have a glass of water/water bottle by your bedside table at night. When you wake up in the morning the first thing you do is drink it. Congrats, you've consumed one of the eight glasses before even getting out of bed.
> Have a glass of water before every meal and between every meal. Assuming you eat three times a day, now you have consumed six glasses right there.
> Have a glass before bed. There's number eight!

I've seen some people get two jugs/bottles of water that will have the capacity of what they need to consume for the day: one bottle for the morning and the other for the afternoon. If they've consumed both jugs then they have consumed their daily intake of water. Try it! Consuming water is vital to improved health and improved appearance. This is truth.

Personal Hygiene

Personal Hygiene – When you look good, you feel good. It is a scientific fact.

I have a Jamaican mother. One of the things that I got to experience, along with many of the other kids who had Jamaican mothers was that when you went out you had to look the part. So many of us first generation Canadians went to school with ribbons, bobbles, and barrettes in our hair – not ribbons, bobbles OR barrettes but ribbons, bobbles AND barrettes – sigh. That was one of the first lessons in taking pride in our appearance. And you could see the pride in our mothers when they took us out and we looked good. We in turn felt good. Russian professional tennis player Maria Sharapova said:

> "When you look good, you feel good. Confidence with what you're wearing is very important. If you feel good, you will always perform your best without worrying about anything."

Now, I can't guarantee that you will not worry about anything if you put on a nice outfit, but, Maria has a point which is backed up by science. Studies show that when an individual feels that he or she looks good on the outside, there is a pep in the step, the person tends to smile more, and has increased confidence. When your confidence level is high, you are more likely to take risks and take action towards your goals/projects. Let's not confuse self-esteem with confidence. You can know that you are really good at something and still suffer with self-esteem issues – many of us do.

But, when you look great and know that you look great, like I said, there is a pep in the step.

Increased confidence in doing a job well done produces increased smiles. When you smile more, it triggers endorphins (feel good hormones) that are released into your brain. This triggers the feel good center in your brain thus making you – FEEL GOOD! So wearing clothes that fit and suit you, taking care of your nails, hair, and teeth – these seem like common sense but these are often areas that are neglected. Taking care of the details often makes the big picture seem clearer.

A few suggestions:

> Nails: If you are like me you could care less about your nails. IT'S TRUE! Sorry, let me rephrase – nails have not been a priority of mine in the past. However, you do not need a French manicure to have clean, cared for nails. Dirty nails communicate a negative image about you and tell your audience you do not care enough about yourself or them to clean your nails. Even more importantly, if you have dirty nails and you are handling food or touching your face – you are more likely to get sick than those who have clean nails. No

one feels good when sick. Common sense.
- ➤ Hair: Keep your hair trimmed, clean and updated. A dated hairstyle screams old fashioned and unclean hair screams neglect. My mother used to tell me that a woman's hair is her crown of glory. Today that crown can be bought at the hair and beauty store for $39.99. No excuses. I love my wigs. My sister-in-law names her wigs – no shame in the game. But in all seriousness, if you feel you do not have time to take care of your hair get a cute short cut or buy some hair to add to your own. But whatever you do – take pride in the care of your hair.
- ➤ Teeth: Look in a mirror before meeting with someone. When people have food in their teeth or bad breath that is all the person you are speaking to can see, smell, or think about. Some of you may need some dental work through no fault of your own. I would love to be able to say that having missing teeth will not matter in your climb to success, however, we live in a superficial society. Don't get me wrong, your level of success is not going to be based on

whether you are missing your front teeth, BUT it does play a role in people's perception of you. That perception is important because no one has become a success totally and completely on their own. If you look at famous or successful people, when they are starting out they may have some dental issues, once they've made it notice that dental work is one of the first things they get done? For instance, Chris Rock, Sporty Spice to name a couple. Whether it is straightening, replacing, or whitening, teeth play a factor in your looks. There are several programs out there to help take care of cavities, replace missing teeth, whiten your teeth etc. Find out about these programs in your community and how you can qualify.

Eat Right

Eat right: Your body is your temple. What you look like in terms of weight is 80 per cent due to your diet. All of the exercise in the world is not going to make a difference if you are eating poorly. The formula to losing weight is simple. Your intake of calories must be LESS than your output of calories. So the energy you expend must be MORE than the calories in the food you consume. It truly is that simple. So, in reality, if you decreased what you ate in terms of portion size, you could possibly lose weight without ever lifting a dumbbell or truly changing your diet. HOWEVER, eating smaller portions of bad foods will not help your body internally, and we are looking for solutions to help the inside AND the outside.

Eating right does not have to be hard either. Go on the internet and search for the foods you like and check out the choices that you have. Then make an informed decision. If you need help, find a dietician, or a nutritionist who can offer some support. Nutritionists and dieticians are there to help and they will coach you through. I'm a huge advocate for hiring people who have studied and are experts in the field that you may need support in. Seeking out help is a good thing – grow your tribe.

Eating well does not have to be expensive, nor does it have to make your head hurt trying to figure out what is what. But I'm here to be truthful with you. Proper eating does require some effort and planning. Here are a few suggestions to help you:

> ➢ Do not eat past 7 p.m. This worked for me. If at all possible, try not to

consume anything other than water past 7pm. If you do have to eat, then make it something light – soup for example. When you eat late, your body has to work hard while you are sleeping (and supposed to be resting) to digest what you have consumed. If you are not resting properly, your body cannot function optimally and then you do not feel good. See how that cycle works? Break it. Also, when you eat late and then go to sleep, digestion is naturally slowed down and much of the food will be stored as fat. Not what we want. One last thing about this: when you stop eating at 7 p.m. (earlier if possible) and then eat breakfast 12 hours later, you kick-start your metabolism. A higher metabolism burns food faster. That is what we want.

- Limit the amount of carbohydrates that you eat. This was a hard one for me. I LOVED BREAD. Check out what a typical spaghetti night looked like for me – Garlic bread (of course) a plate full of pasta (of course) a salad with croutons, and then some sort of cake for dessert. Carb overload? And I could not understand why I could not get rid of my gut. I tried to blame my little gut on the fact that I had three children but if I'm honest, I've always had a little gut – even BEFORE I ever got pregnant. Further, I could not understand why my stomach would often look like I was about six months pregnant. NO JOKE. I had people ask me when I was due – and I wasn't even pregnant. Not good for the self-esteem. But you know what? When you cut bread out of your diet it's amazing how the bloatedness that many of us feel just goes away! I suggest reading the book Wheat Belly – it will totally enlighten you on this topic. When I stopped eating bread (wheat specifically) and started purchasing gluten free pasta, the bloatedness went away. The uneasy feeling went away. The extreme fatigue went away and a feeling of lightness came over me. I had more energy and my stomach went way down. I always know when I've eaten bread because my waistline on the pants I'm wearing gets tighter.

> Figure out your snack foods before you need to snack. How often are your days filled with running from one place to

another? Then you realize you are hungry and all you have are fast food choices? Determine what snack you want before you get to that point. Pack it the night before and snack on that instead of stopping for fast food. Hey, it will not only save your waistline but it will save you some money too! A friend of mine did an experiment with this and he found that by planning his snacks – meaning purchasing them at the grocery store and packing them daily – he saved a whopping $30/week. This is $120 per month, which is a savings of $1440 per year. What could you do with an extra $1440 this year?

Undergarments

Undergarments: What you wear under your clothing is as important as what you wear on the outside. When I was young there was this joke that mothers told their children – make sure you are wearing nice underwear because you may get hit by a bus and you don't want the doctors to see you in messed up undies. I know, CRAZY. But in all seriousness, your undergarments help clothing fall well and help give you the professional look you desire.

Check out the difference. It looks as though the figure on the left had a breast lift right? A really good bra may be a bit more expensive; however, it will last longer and make you look like you have a longer and slimmer torso.

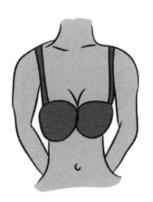

For those of us who have had gravity play with that area of our bodies, a good bra can make all the difference. As mentioned, when you feel you look good, and I mean really good, you know you look good and you naturally walk with confidence. You become bolder.

Wearing a bra that lifts and has smooth edges as well as comfortable panties with the invisible edge helps make you look well put together. This in turn is what you will communicate subconsciously – I'm put together.

Men, wear boxers or underwear that are comfortable and fitted. Wear a t-shirt under your dress shirt. I should mention – make it a t-shirt that does not have designs on it. That way it's not appearing through your dress shirt. There is nothing funnier than a man who is wearing a dress shirt and the print of Mickey Mouse or Millers Lite is showing through – not cool – funny, but not cool.

Know Your Body Shape

Know your Body Shape. Knowledge is power. Knowing what looks good on your body helps in knowing what clothes and accessories to buy. The key to any great look is to create the illusion of balance. Our brains naturally look for symmetry. So, if you have wide hips and small shoulders, you want to wear clothing that creates the illusion of wider shoulders and smaller hips.

The ideal shape is the hourglass because it is evenly proportioned. Whether a small hourglass or an extra lovely hourglass, the size does not matter. It is the shape. Most hourglasses can wear almost anything and look fabulous. The banana/straight body type does not have much shape and therefore to create the illusion will wear clothing with belts to bring in the waist line or wear color block clothing.

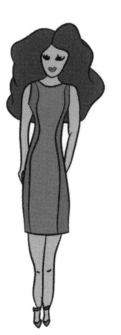

This look is the best look for a banana/straight shaped female because it creates the illusion of an hourglass. It creates the illusion of shape and symmetry.

The pear/bell, has a larger bottom than top. This shaped woman should wear darker colors on the bottom – skirts, pants, shorts, and lighter colors on top. She will also wear accent necklaces to draw the eye up. Tops with a wider neckline will provide the illusion of width. Longer tops will also elongate her look. Tops should also hit above or below the widest part of the hip – not **on** the widest part of the hip. A-line skirts are also very flattering.

The Apple/Triangle shaped woman has wide shoulders and a narrow hip. She will want to wear brighter colors on the bottom and more subtle colors on the top. Essentially the opposite of the Pear/Bell. The empire waist is a good look on this beauty.

Apples tend to have a great chest and great legs and a full middle. You will want to bring focus up or down but away from the midsection. Clothing line should be straight or slightly fitted with fabrics being soft.

Invest in a consult with a stylist – even if it is only one appointment. During this appointment find out your body shape, and what style clothes look best on you.

Know Your Undertone

Know your Undertone. This is equally as important as knowing your body shape because knowing your undertone will allow you to know what colors look best on you. Undertone, in laymen's terms, is the hue underneath your skin. Some people refer to it as yellow undertone or pink undertone. You may have heard of it called warm or cool. However, it makes a big difference when you know how to dress according to your undertone.

Have you ever been out and you look in the mirror and you look tired or drained but you feel great? Or have you ever been asked by well-meaning friends/co-workers – are you feeling ok today? You look a little tired? But you feel fully energized? The reason for this would be because of undertone. Wearing the right colors can make you sizzle or make you fade into the background. Figuring out your undertone is simple and will help make getting dressed in the morning easy-peasy!

People with a yellow/warm undertone tend to look best in beige/off white as opposed to bright white. Whereas people with a pink/cool undertone look great in bright white. It is difficult to tell you what colors are going to be best on you because in addition to your undertone, you need to keep in account your hair and eye color (which changes regularly for many) so I'm going to tell you how to determine your skin undertone and give you a VERY generalized idea of what colors look best on you.

> Helpful hint to figure out your undertone – look at your veins in your arms (wrists). Are they bluish in color or are they greenish in color? Your veins are naturally blue. If they are bluish then you likely have a pink or a neutral undertone. The colors that are going to look best on you are bright whites, and cool colors like blue and green. If your veins are greenish it is because you have a yellow undertone (blue + yellow = green). You will likely

look great in off white/ivory, beige, warm tones like reds, yellows, orange. Each color has a variety of hues – this is a total and complete other conversation – but when shopping ask the clerk to show you clothing in warm tones or cool tones. Try them and check the difference. Makes all the difference in looking good, and looking great!

Again, I recommend, like in tip #6 that you have at least one or two sessions with a stylist. This is what they do and what they love. Their goal is to ensure you look great. Once you have the knowledge, you will have it forever. A great investment – try it!

Exercise

Exercise – So important. Get your body moving. Get your blood circulating. Get that heart pumping! Exercising will help you with your concentration, digestion, sleep, mood, and body image. You do not have to be a gym enthusiast, all you need is 20min per day of increased activity to get your heart pumping. Walk briskly. This is a minimum. Studies show that by walking for twenty minutes a day it releases those endorphins we discussed above.

Check out the definition of an endorphin by everydayhealth.com[10]:

> **Endorphin** is a combination of the words "endogenou" (produced within the body) and "morphine" They're released from the pituitary gland of the brain during periods of strenuous exercise, emotional stress, pain, and orgasm. **Endorphins** help relieve pain and induce feelings of pleasure or euphoria.

Who doesn't want to feel pleasure and euphoria?

According to the Mayo Clinic, the health benefits of regular exercise and physical activity range from boosting your mood to improving your sex life[11]. Yes, it's true! When I make exercise a part of my daily routine, I truly feel like I'm on top of the world. Ok, maybe a bit dramatic, but I do feel good. Really it only takes 20-30 minutes of activity per day to make

---

[10] Konkel, L. (2015, October 16). What are endorphins? *Everyday Health*. Retrieved from:
http://www.everydayhealth.com/endorphins/guide/

[11] Exercise: 7 benefits of regular physical activity. *Mayo Clinic*. Retrieved from: http://www.mayoclinic.org/healthy-lifestyle/fitness/in-depth/exercise/art-20048389

a difference in your mood, your physical appearance, and your energy level!

Regular exercise helps prevent or manage a wide range of health problems and concerns as well. Problems such as stroke, metabolic syndrome, type 2 diabetes, depression, a number of types of cancer, arthritis and falls. Would you not agree that preventing these diseases/health issues would be much easier and much more enjoyable than having to intervene after the fact?

We live in a time where inactivity is the norm. Where being overweight is the norm. Where taking care of the symptoms of disease is the norm. This rings especially true in North America. If you really want to Finesse your Life - Body and live your best life now you WILL take 20-30 minutes of your day and do something – anything – just get moving. Walk, run, swim, get on a cardio machine but do something. For myself, I know it will take a lot for me to go to the gym. I know this about myself – primarily because I'm a single parent and to find child care to go to the gym is not on my priority list. BUT that does not mean I can't exercise. In the warmer months I will go on walks with the kids – they love it because we get to spend quality time together. I walk and they talk, talk, talk, and talk some more. It's really pretty comical. In the winter, I may go up and down my steps or get on the stationary bike. I will park extra far in parking lots or take the stairs. Every little bit helps.

The hardest part about exercising is just starting. At least it is for me. Once I'm doing it, I like it. Probably because of the endorphin release thing. So make exercising part of your daily routine. If you have to wake up a little earlier to fit it in then do so. Let's have a serious moment – if your health is not good then you will not be able to participate in life the way you want. Pure and simple. Exercise is a preventative measure for disease and a means to make you feel good immediately. What do I often say? When you feel better you think better, you do better. It's not just talk, its truth – take care of your body.

Here is my suggestion to implement this tip:

> ➢ Schedule in your exercise time and make it a priority. When it is written down you are more likely to do it. Find 20 to 30 minutes per day to do some form of physical activity.

Sleep

Sleep – Your body, like all other creatures and machines on this earth, needs to recharge. The best time for your body to do this is when you are asleep. Tissues repair, mind is at rest, and you have more energy. Again, you feel good, you look good, you think good; you do _____ - fill in the blank.

The amount of sleep that you need per day varies from person to person. Most experts will say that in order for your body to fully recharge you need a good 7-9 hours of sleep per day. The exact number is really dependent on you. I know that I feel lethargic if I sleep more than 8hrs per day. It's almost like I overslept. I tend to function well if I get 7hrs of sleep.

Did you know that we spend 1/3 of our lives sleeping? That's a lot! That also tells us that it is important. So just some suggestions to help you get the best sleep:

> ➢ Turn the computer/phone/electronics off at least an hour before you are going to go to sleep. The blue light from electronics can mess with what is called our circadian rhythm or our sleep/wake cycle. This cycle naturally tells our body when to sleep and when

to be awake. Not a great thing to mess with!
- ➢ Avoid caffeine before going to bed. Caffeine will rob you of rest and keeps your heart rate up when it needs to relax to get into a good sleep rhythm.
- ➢ Turn off all lights and loud noises. You may think that you need music or other noises to soothe you to sleep, however, sound will stimulate the brain thus robbing the brain of its needed rest.
- ➢ Get your finances in order. Yep, you read correctly. Get your finances in order. One of the biggest robbers of sleep for people is the worry of their finances. Best advice I can give on this one – you do not necessarily need to make more money but you do need to live within your means. Understand the role money plays and that it is used as a tool. Once you understand or gather knowledge about money, then you can decide whether your income needs to increase and then you can start to build wealth.

Good Posture

Good posture – Sit up! Stand up! Shoulders back! It matters! Let me ask you something. Has your head ever turned to look at someone who was sleuthing their way into a room? Head down, shoulders hunched, not making any eye contact with anyone? It's just not attractive. It does not relay that you have confidence and it's physically bad for you. It's true! Sitting up with your back straight helps your spine – slouching hurts your spine. Also, your bodily functions work better when your posture is better. Listen, I can't make this stuff up! It is so true.

According to the Greatist team[12]:

When you slouch or slump, so does your spine, leading to bad circulation. This can cause vertebrae to deteriorate over time. Chronic fatigue can also result. Coupled with circulation issues, the result can be early exhaustion. Chronic back, neck, and shoulder pain can also result from the strain of bad positioning. Fifty percent of working Americans suffer from back pain, and it's the second most common reason for doctor visits. Twenty five percent of those with back pain suffer from a herniated disc, which may be caused by poor posture.

Sit up, chest out has a whole new meaning doesn't it?

---

[12] The ultimate guide to good posture. (2011, November 28) Greatist. Retrieved from: https://greatist.com/health/ultimate-guide-good-posture

Suggestions:

> To accomplish correct posture you will need to be mindful of your posture. Throughout the day check in with yourself. Are you slouching? Create a reminder on your handheld device to remind you of when to check in with yourself.
> Let people around you know what you are doing and ask them to nudge you if you are slouching. A little nudge here and there never hurt!

RECAP:

Ten tips:

1. Acceptance
2. Drink Water
3. Personal Hygiene
4. Eat Right
5. Undergarments
6. Know Your Body Shape
7. Know Your Undertone
8. Exercise
9. Sleep
10. Good posture

Which two can you start with?

_____
_____
_____
_____

I believe in changing small and changing often to create lasting change. I will be accountable to myself and to [insert your coach/accountability partner's name]
_____
__ with regards to my commitment to Finesse my Life – Body.

For each goal I will write down HOW I will implement the goal, WHEN I will implement the goal, WHAT my expectation and desired outcome is for the goal, and WHY this goal is important to me.

Remember, change small change often. Start with two and add as time goes on.

Starting on [insert date]
_____ I will implement these two goals.

1._____
_____
_____
_____
_____

_____
_____
_____
_____
_____
_____
_____
_____
_____
_____
_____
_____
_____
_____
_____
_____

_____

Record your success daily.

2._____
_____
_____
_____
_____
_____
_____
_____
_____
_____

_____
_____
_____
_____
_____
_____
_____
_____

_____

Record your success daily.

As I begin to achieve my goals I will implement the other tips to add to my success!

3.

_____
_____
_____
_____
_____
_____
_____
_____
_____
_____
_____
_____

_____
_____
_____
_____
_____
_____
_____
_____
_____

Record your success daily.

4._____
_____
_____
_____
_____
_____
_____
_____
_____
_____
_____
_____
_____
_____
_____
_____

_____
_____
_____

_____

Record your success daily.

5._____
_____
_____
_____
_____
_____
_____
_____
_____
_____
_____
_____
_____
_____
_____
_____
_____
_____

_____

Record your success daily.

6._____

_____
_____
_____
_____
_____
_____
_____
_____
_____
_____
_____
_____
_____
_____
_____
_____
_____
_____
_____
_____

_____

Record your success daily.

7._____

_____
_____
_____
_____
_____

Record your success daily.

8. _____

_____

Record your success daily.

9._____

_____
_____
_____

Record your success daily.

10._____
_____
_____
_____
_____
_____
_____
_____
_____
_____
_____
_____
_____
_____
_____
_____
_____
_____

Record your success daily.

Finesse Your Life – Spirit

Never underestimate the power of dreams and the influence of the human spirit. We are all the same in this notion: The potential for greatness lives within each of us. - Wilma Rudolph

Whether spiritual or not, many people cannot deny that as human beings, we are made up of more than just organs, bones, and outward physical characteristics. We each have a spirit. A unique something that makes us who we are. An inner being. This inner being is what drives us. It's like the engine of a car. The car isn't going anywhere without the engine. Just as we are not going anywhere without our spirit. In some of us our spirit, the essence of who we are, is strong. It is vibrant! It is seen and felt in the joy that is exuded from us. However, in others, the spirit is weak or weary. Often this happens in people who have been beat down emotionally over and over again. These people look tired and weary, they are sad, and probably not the most fun to be around. However, the spirit never dies. It cannot die. It is energy and it is constantly in movement. It may be diminished, it may be flickering, but it does not die. Even when the human body dies, the spirit lives on – whether you believe in heaven, reincarnation, or another form of after life, the spirit continues to live after our bodies cease.

I can distinctly remember the first time I truly experienced a death of someone around me and then again when I experienced the death of someone close to me. I distinctly remember going to the funerals and walking into the viewing room. With viewing of the person who I knew of, I remember hearing the comments people would say about her. How they were fun loving, how they were full of life, or how they always had something smart to say. I remember going to view the body and it was just that – a body. There was no life, no exuberance but I could sense the awesomeness in that person in the room. Her spirit lived on. I then remember when my uncle passed away. I watched him die. He had cancer. He was an uncle that was around for the birth of my mother and my birth, and the birth of my own children. I remember the jokes he would always tell. I remember stealing his cigarettes to prevent him from smoking and throwing the cigarettes down the sewer. He never got mad at me, but would just give me a look, shake his head, and laugh. When he passed away – it was not him. I watched him as his spirit faded.

He was such a strong man and in the end it was like his body betrayed him. However, his spirit did not die. His body did. I watched as his spirit left him but IT DID NOT DIE. It is a surreal feeling and a surreal experience. I tear up at the thought but what it made me realize is that we ALL have a spirit that will never die. Our spirits, as mentioned, are energy that we leave with our loved ones and lives on in the stories told about us long after we physically leave this earth. My intention here is not to convert you from whatever belief system you have, but simply to have you realize that the human spirit is real and it needs to be taken care of. It is the energy we leave behind and it takes purposeful and focused and protective work to take care of our spirits.

So how do we help our spirit to burn strong and bright? How do we keep the spirit healthy and vibrant? We do it by loving ourselves. We do it by loving and taking care of ourselves. We do it by implementing the next ten tips to really Finesse Your Spirit.

Gratefulness

Gratefulness – Being truly grateful for everything that happens in your life seems like an impossible task. There are things that happen to us that seem so unfair and so cruel that the thought of feeling grateful for it seems ridiculous right? But being grateful is necessary. Everything that happens in life shapes who we are right now. All of the good and all of the not so good. I read something written by Robert Emmons[13], a researcher of the effects of gratitude, which stuck with me:

> ...gratitude makes us appreciate the value of something, and when we appreciate the value of something, we extract more benefits from it; we're less likely to take it for granted.

How often have we done that? Taken things, people, relationships for granted? I remember a period in my life where I struggled financially. It was during the recession experienced in the 2000s, I believe it was 2008. My husband at the time had lost his job. He had a pretty good paying job making about $60,000 per year. We went from a household annual income of over $120,000 to living solely off of my income. We were able to make it work for a few months but then things got really tight. Then we had to start selling stuff. Looking back we made some poor financial decisions in our effort to get out

---

[13] Emmons, R. (2010, November 16). Why gratitude is good. Greater Good. Retrieved from:
http://greatergood.berkeley.edu/article/item/why_gratitude_is_good/

of what felt like a drowning ship. In the end, we crawled out of it. But that experience taught me a few valuable lessons.

1. Never believe that *things* are as valuable as *people*. When you have to sell things you quickly realize how unimportant they are. It was my family and close friends that helped us keep our house not the things that were in it!

2. Be prepared. One thing I know is that I will never be broke again. The day I did not know where I was going to find money to buy formula for my baby was the lowest day of my life. I vowed never to be there again. Preparing financially for hiccups is crucial (as you will read further on in the tips).

3. Giving of yourself and your resources in your most desperate time of need is the most satisfying feeling there is. Although that time of my life was incredibly stressful and super humbling, I am grateful for it. Grateful for the lessons and grateful for the experience. It's made me a stronger person and a more empathetic person. Showing gratitude for what you have, what you don't have, what you will have – it's all necessary so that we can appreciate it. When someone thanks you for something you did – big or small – how do you

feel? Kinda good inside right? You smile right? It's a springboard to a snowball effect of gratitude and positivity.

When I was a beauty consultant for Mary Kay Cosmetics, one of the daily tasks was to write down six things that we were most grateful for. It did not have to be specifically about Mary Kay and it was encouraged to think of things you are grateful for outside of Mary Kay. So on a daily basis we were tasked with writing down the six things that we were most grateful for that day. Mary Kay Ash was a brilliant woman who really was the picture of someone who fed her spirit and her mind and shared herself with thousands of others. She is responsible for helping thousands of women pick themselves up out of poverty, abusive relationships, self discovery etc... She suffered tremendous losses from a failed marriage, death of a child, business losses and yet, she showed up daily to encourage others to rise above their circumstances. Her story is an amazing one and her business mind is studied in Harvard business schools. I guess she knew something about this gratefulness thing.

Some keys to help you with your gratefulness journey are:

- Before stepping out of bed say out loud what you are grateful for. It will immediately put you in a good mood and start your day on the right foot.
- Write down at least three things that you are most grateful for everyday and express gratitude for it.
- At least once a day let someone know that you appreciate them. It will not only put a spring in their step but it will put a spring in your step too!

Reflection

Reflection – being able to reflect on your life is great and sounds "deep" and in some ways it is fairly "deep". To be truly reflective means to be honest with yourself. Can you do that? Some of us have a hard time with that. Why? Well, it can be difficult to look at yourself and not be happy with what you see. We all make mistakes, but for some people, it is very difficult to be able to admit to those mistakes or even to take responsibility for those mistakes.

Google defines self-reflection as "meditation or serious thought about one's character, actions, and motives." Are you able to really take a look at your character? Your actions? Your motives? If you believe yes, are you able to see the good and where you can do better? Are you able to admit that your motives for your actions were genuine or can you admit that they may have been self-serving? These may seem like harsh questions, but they are not. They are real questions. Questions that we need to be able to ask ourselves so that by the end of the day, you are able to put your head to pillow and believe that you did your best that day. And if you are not able to say you did your best, then you are able to figure out how you can do better the next day. This is an important exercise because the belief you have about yourself will tremendously impact your peace of mind and your success level in life. Remember, it all starts with belief.

The art of self-reflection is simply using the tools you use every day to observe and analyze. We do this daily with everything around us. We have to in order to get through the day. We gather information, examine it, and then make a decision as to what to do with the information. We do this at work, we do this when we offer advice to others, and we do this in picking out our clothes for the day! The issue is that many of us do not use these same tools to observe and analyze *ourselves*. Remember what we discussed in the first section of this book about being more aware of ourselves and those around us? Of being able to manage our own behaviors and the relationships that we are in? This is self-reflection. Introspection involves examining one's own thoughts, feelings and sensations in order to gain insight[14].

In order to successfully self-reflect you have to be able to be still. You need to have sufficient time to reflect and process the information that you will learn or observe about yourself. What you will gain from being more reflective is vital to your personal success in life and in business.

I read an article that actually listed seven benefits of being self-reflective:

- You will notice the negative patterns in your life. Once you are aware of them then you can change them.
- Keeps you focused on the bigger picture
- Keeps you focused on what is within your control
- Allows you to better face your fears

---

[14] Uzer, S. (2015, March 6). 7 ways self-reflection and introspection will give you a happier life. Elite Daily. Retrieved from: http://elitedaily.com/life/7-ways-self-reflection-introspection-will-give-happier-life/943309/

- Allows you to define what happiness means to you
- Allows you to make decisions based on your conscious
- Will allow you to get different results

Could you see the benefit of becoming more self-reflective? Could you see how your life could improve? I'm not going to try to make you think that your life will suddenly become glorious when you start looking at yourself more deeply. You may discover things that upset you or make you feel uncomfortable. HOWEVER, that process is necessary in order to get to the other side. Too often we want to shy away from things that make us uncomfortable. However, if we use the analogy of giving birth – ladies you will relate, men you can empathize – for ten months we prepare for the baby that we are carrying. We take the vitamins, we see the doctor, and we do what we are supposed to do in order to prepare for the baby. We are happy (most of the time). Then the pains start. It's time to birth the baby. It hurts, we want to take meds to sooth the pain. We don't want to feel the pain, but the discomfort is necessary in order to birth the baby. The discomfort is necessary to signal us that it is time to give birth. Then, once the baby is born, the pain is forgotten and our lives are forever changed.

When we adopt the process of self-reflection, we have to understand that prior to analyzing ourselves, we did what we knew to do in order to survive and thrive. We lived by that prescription I wrote about in section one. When we self-reflect it's like the contractions – it can be painful – but afterwards, our lives are changed – for the better!

Are you screaming "Tell me how!"? Well let's start simple:

> - Be still. Take time to be still and then ask yourself these questions: How do I feel about this morning? Throughout the day you can ask yourself how you feel about your day. After making a major decision, take a few minutes and ask yourself how you feel about the decision you made. How did you feel about the process you went through to make the decision? When a difficult situation comes up and you have resolved the issue, how do you feel about the manner in which you managed the situation? In everything, just do these check ins. Whatever your response – I feel good, or I feel I could have done better, or I do not feel comfortable with how I managed that –

whatever the response, then probe deeper and provide some evidence for your feelings. You know in school how the teachers taught us to start with the idea, then provide the evidence to prove the idea. Same thing – if you feel good about something *why* do you feel good? What about the process produced benefit? Or alternatively, what about the process made you uncomfortable? In other words, analyze you. At first this may seem tedious but once you make this a part of your routine and take the time out to do some reflecting of self – you will become more attune, and more honest with yourself. This is your goal. Simply just taking an honest look at how you react and how you think about certain situations. This simple act (didn't say easy) helps you to know you more. Being self-aware (as mentioned in the previous section) is imperative to being able to manage yourself and ultimately your move up on the success ladder.

➢ Do multiple check ins with yourself throughout the day. You want to get to a point where you are able to know yourself so well that you can make decisions simpler, easier, and wiser.

Positive Affirmations

Positive affirmations. What are you telling you about who you want to be, going to be, or simply who you really are right now? We were all born with greatness within us. We all have the potential to live a vibrant and successful life however we define that to be. But like everything else, you have to believe in yourself and that greatness in order for it to become a reality.

Although thinking positively is important, hearing positive statements about yourself is also important. Let me ask you something. Think about the last time you were sitting with someone and they were complimenting you on a job well done. In the midst of the compliments, they make a suggestion for you to change one thing. What do you remember more? The compliments or the critique? Most people remember and concentrate on the critique more than the compliments. The reason why is because our brains remember the negative more than they remember the positive.

Professor Nass, a co-author of "The Man Who Lied to His Laptop: What Machines Teach Us

About Human Relationships", wrote an article in the New York Times where he stated that the brain handles positive and negative information in different hemispheres[15]. He wrote that negative emotions involve more thinking and the information is processed more thoroughly than positive emotions. Therefore, people tend to ruminate more about unpleasant events and will use stronger words to describe than then they do happy ones.

Due to the fact that we have a natural tendency to think and ruminate on negative events and feelings, it is vital that we counteract this tendency with positivity. Positive affirmations are defined as "...the practice
of positive thinking and self-empowerment—fostering a belief that "a positive mental attitude supported by affirmations will achieve success in anything."

I remember when I was nineteen years old, I went for an interview at a modelling agency. The lady that I met with was nice – and brutally honest. I remember making sure I was dressed to the Ts! I had on some fitted white jeans, a fitted yet loose top, heels, my hair was

---

[15] Nass, C and Yen, C. (2010). *The Man Who Lied to His Laptop: What We Can Learn About Ourselves from Our Machines*. London, England : Penguin Books, Ltd.

naturally long at that time and it was pressed and styled perfectly. I had on colored contact lenses (it was the in thing back then – don't judge) and my makeup was done modestly. I have to admit, I looked great! So I was pretty confident when I walked into the room. We sat and we talked about the experiences I had in modelling and what I hoped to get out of it. I indicated that I wanted to be in print/editorial shoots and do some runway. She proceeded to tell me that I was too short for runway (5'7" and ¾), she said that I had tall gums (gummy smile – don't go back and look at my pics to see if that's true – LOL) and she said I'd have to lose ten pounds (I was only about 130lbs and according to my mother – too skinny). Do you think I can tell you one positive thing the woman said? I know she said some positive things but I don't remember. But I sure as heck remember the negative. Now, I didn't end up pursuing modelling – not because of this lady but because it's just not the path I chose. But 22yrs later, I can still remember her face and the critiques she said to me. I had a choice - let this crush me or keep it moving. I chose to keep it moving. I still modelled locally and I've perfected my smile (which I am very happy with) but my point is this – remembering the negative is easy. Focusing on the positive takes purposeful work. In order to put myself out in the world in the ways that I do means that I have had to tell myself I'm attractive, I am a beautiful person inside and out, I love people and people love me. If you are living and if you are interacting with people, you will face criticism. Some valid, some not. YOU have to believe in yourself and your abilities. Tell yourself you are great and then simply BE GREAT.

The point of tip 3 is this – although the brain will process and appreciate the positive it is easier for it to focus on the negative. Therefore, we just have to be a bit more purposeful in telling ourselves positive messages so that it will stick. Here are some ideas how:

- ➢ When you wake up, look in the mirror, smile, and tell yourself who you are. Whether you feel it or not – tell yourself who you are. Feelings are fleeting they go up and down depending on your mood. Fact is fact. You are great. There is greatness within you and you have a unique gift to offer this world. Remind yourself of this daily.

> Change the negative talk to positive talk. Talk about what you *can* do as opposed to what you *cannot* do.
> Be mindful of what you are saying about yourself. Really watch the "I am" statements. Ensure that whatever you are saying about yourself is positive.

Replenish

Replenish – what do you enjoy doing? I mean really enjoy doing? For some people it's sleeping. For others it is reading. For others it's sex. Whatever it is – if this is what helps to rejuvenate you than you need to do more of it! I think I just got real popular! But seriously, out of a 24hr period, taking at least 30-60 minutes on your own to zone out and take care of yourself is not too much to ask or expect.

I wrote this speech once where I talked about not being able to help someone else with your cup that runneth over because it is in fact an empty cup. When you give, and give, and give of yourself without taking time to fill yourself up, you run the risk of breakdown. What happens when a car runs out of gas? It cannot operate. What happens when a cell phone loses battery life? The apps slow down and the phone eventually shuts down. What happens when you go, go, go and do not take time to rest and rejuvenate – enjoy life? You will slow down, you will not be as alert, you will become anxious and you run the risk of a break down. Taking some time to replenish is worth preventing problems from occurring because to intervene once a health issue has arisen is much harder and time consuming than preventing it from happening in the first place.

My mother is a perfect example of the above. Ever since I was a baby I can remember her just going, going, going. She would work full time, take care of my sister and myself, be involved in the community, help take care of her extended family, go above and beyond for her students and the list goes on and on. When she was in her mid-fifties she had a mild heart attack. She was not excessively overweight and her health was seemingly good, but one thing she rarely ever did was take time for herself. The stress of life and the lack of self-care showed itself through her heart. Her body told her – we are not going to put up with this anymore so something has got to give. After the heart attack the mere thought of returning to a classroom – a profession she loved – caused her anxiety. Until this day, my mother becomes anxious with the slightest issue. She's an amazing woman – don't get me wrong but the continued stress of life, the continued giving of self, without taking time to care for herself has created a situation where she becomes very anxious, very easily. She has been forced to take better care of herself but the toll of not caring for her spirit for over 30 years has made some lasting impressions on her psyche. Provide yourself with an opportunity to prevent as opposed to intervene. Here are some strategies how:

> ➢ Schedule you time and honor it. Find at least 60 minutes in your day to do something you really enjoy. If you have to break up the 60 minutes than do that, but schedule time. You are just as much a priority – if not more – than that business meeting, that date, that errand. You cannot give from your cup that runneth over if your cup is empty.
> ➢ If you are anything like I was, you may have actually forgotten what you enjoy to do. One summer a friend of mine asked me what I like to do for fun. I could not answer the question. I had spent so much time for so long just being busy that I no longer knew what I did for fun for myself. I had to relearn me. I had to think about what makes me smile/laugh and does not require me to exert brain power to think.

For me, spending time with friends and hanging out, or spending time with my kids at the park were the things I came up with at first. But then there are times I really enjoy just being by myself and reading a book, going for a walk or watching Netflix. I'm not hard to please – LOL. What do you like to do that requires very little energy expended?

_____
_____
_____
_____.

Release

Release –Although seemingly similar to forgiveness, release means to let go of the things you cannot control. Release means to not dwell. Release means to appreciate where you are and what you are doing right now. Live in the moment – not in the past and not in the future but in the immediate moment. Admittedly, this was a hard one for me. As I wrote previously, I would dwell on the negative and remember every criticism. I had a real issue with wanting people to like me and so if I felt as though someone did not like me I would dwell on it. Spend a lot of time trying to figure out what I could do to get them to change their mind. I mean, let's be honest. No one enjoys being disliked, but there comes a point where you have to say I am who I am whether you like me or not. Then be comfortable with who you are and know you add value to this world. Simple. Not easy. But simple.

I had a friend who had a need to be in control of everything around her. She needed to be in control of her child's schedule, of her husband's whereabouts, of any project we would work on together. She was a micromanager – argh! One of her major issues in our work together was that she constantly needed to know who was in support of our projects. When she found out who was not supporting one of our endeavors, those people would go on an imaginary black list. Meaning, she would follow who they would support and then dwell on why they would not support our endeavors. Then she would come up with hypothesis as to why people did not want to support our endeavors. Then, when she could not figure that out she would try to get me to ask the people why they were not being supportive. It was exhausting. Eventually I had to say to her – Let it go! Focus on what we can control and let's keep it moving. Although easier said than done, releasing that feeling of having to control everything is so freeing! For some people this is easy to do, they just move on. For others, it takes implementing strategies to be able to keep it moving. Here are some ways to do it;

- ➤ Play the tape until the end. When something is bothering you and you are not able to shake it play the tape until the end. Meaning, provide a hypothesis with regards to what is going to happen in the worst case scenario. Typically what is actually going to happen and what you think is going to happen are not that closely related. Worrying is simply a negative form of meditation. It has never ever solved anything. Let me ask you, what is the purpose of worrying and what will the outcome be because you spent time worrying? Nothing positive I'm sure. Release it.
- ➤ Let it go. Whatever the issue, drop it. Do not worry about it. Do not dwell on it. Just let it go. This takes work. You will have to remind yourself to let it go frequently. When you find yourself thinking of whatever is bothering you then you will have to follow it up immediately with I'm letting this go. Then think of something positive – fairies and stardust if that's what

makes you smile. But counteract the negative with positive. Works every time. Warning: At first you may have to do this frequently throughout your day. Don't worry, it does get easier and less frequent as time goes on.

Prayer & Meditation
Prayer & Meditation – No matter your religious or spiritual belief, prayer and meditation are part of the rejuvenation process. As I was doing research about the connection between the brain and prayer and meditation, I came across studies that are being done in the USA and Canada specifically about understanding what happens in the brains and bodies of people who believe they connect with the divine. This field of study is called Neurotheology. Studies are showing that the brains of people who spend hours in prayer and meditation are different than those who do not. Remember that saying what you think about you bring about? Essentially, this statement is stating that what you focus on more you tend to bring about into your life. A neuroscientist named Andrew Newberg from the University of Pennsylvania has spent a significant amount of time scanning the brains of religious people. What he has found is

this[16]: "The more you focus on something — whether that's math or auto racing or football or God — the more that becomes your reality, the more it becomes written into the neural connections of your brain," [17]

Study after study today shows that increased stress levels have a negative impact on our health. There is a correlation between high stress levels and the increased rate of disease in our society. Prayer and meditation help to decrease those stress levels and therefore are being slated as remedies for stress. Further, according to a University of Rochester study, prayer is more effective than taking herbs or pursuing other nontraditional healing methods. Dr. Newberg has found that prayer and meditation increase our dopamine levels which is associated with states of wellbeing and joy[18].

People who have hope and a belief in a higher power are more optimistic about life. That optimism is the difference between life and

---

[16] Hagerty, B. B. (2009, March 20). Prayer may reshape your brain...and your reality. NPR: The Science of Spirituality. Retrieved from: http://www.npr.org/templates/story/story.php?storyId=104310443

[17] White, R. (2015) *Your Brain on God: How prayer affects memory.* Retrieved from: https://memorise.org/brain-articles/brain-god-prayer-affects-memory

[18] Schiffman, R. (2012, January 18). Why people who pray are healthier than those who don't. *Huffington Post.* Retrieved from: http://www.huffingtonpost.com/richard-schiffman/why-people-who-pray-are-heathier_b_1197313.html

death sometimes – no joke. Taking time to spend praying and meditating is time taken to recharge your battery so that you can live the best you.

Suggestions:

> Schedule prayer/meditation time. Wake up a little earlier and spend that time in prayer. Spend that time being thankful/grateful for what you have and where you are in life. The bible says to start your day in prayer. It allows you to be still, to seek guidance in how to get through your day, and to start your day positively.
> Pray throughout the day. Prayer is speaking to your higher power. For me, that higher power is God. I can respect that not everyone shares my belief. However, most people believe in something. Take time throughout your day and speak to your higher power – be thankful, seek guidance, and feel the calm of knowing you have a higher power looking out for you. Prayer does not have to last for hours, you can pray for half a minute if that's what you need to do throughout the

day. But use your time wisely to be still and pray/meditate.

Family & Loved Ones

Family/loved ones – Surrounding yourself or staying connected to family whether blood related or not is important to keeping your spirit strong. Family is anyone you love and who loves you. Creating an environment with positive family members around you helps to enhance your sense of belonging, helps your self-esteem, and helps you learn the true meaning of love. Love is patient, love is kind. It does not envy, it does not boast, it is not proud. It does not dishonor others, it is not self-seeking, it is not easily angered, it keeps no record of wrongs. Love does not delight in evil but rejoices with the truth. It always protects, always trusts, always hopes, always perseveres (Bible).

To love someone and be loved has no boundaries of blood lines.

There are three people in this world that I would tell anything to, who I trust implicitly, and who I know loves me unconditionally. Two of these people are blood related, one is not. It is important to have people in your life who are close to you. They are like God's angels that he sends to you. True family will not be afraid to celebrate your wins and your losses. They will be there to help wipe up the messes we sometimes get ourselves in and they will be there to congratulate you when you do well.

The people that I am talking about in this tip are your most inner circle. People you trust.

In USA today, Marilyn Elias wrote that psychologists say that one of the things that makes people genuinely happy is to surround themselves by friends and family and do things with them on a regular basis. [19]

Your inner circle of friends and family are the ones that accept you for who you really are. You do not have to put on a show, you do not have to be on your best behavior, you simply have to be you in your total raw self. If you do not have people like this in your life, take your time in finding them. However just know, there are people who want what is best for you without any type of compensation for themselves. So this relationship would not be a coach or someone you have hired to cheer you on along the way but someone who is there for

---

[19] Elias, M. (2002, December 12). Psychologist now know what makes people happy. *USA Today*. Retrieved from: http://usatoday30.usatoday.com/news/health/2002-12-08-happy-main_x.htm

you because they want to be. Filling your spirit with love is key to keeping it strong and vibrant.

Nature

Nature – Most people can see the beauty in nature, some of us hate to be outdoors. But soaking in the sights, sounds, and smells of Mother Nature can be both gratifying and relaxing. It can be soothing and reinvigorating. Whether being active outdoors or just sitting on a bench and soaking it all in, being in nature can feed your spirit.

In a study led by Gregory Bratman of Stanford University, he wrote that time in nature was found to have a positive effect on mood and aspects of cognitive function, including working memory, as well as a dampening effect on anxiety[20]. Something I have said to clients, to my social media following, and now to you – when you feel good you do good. It's commonsense. Taking a time out to enjoy nature helps with many of the tips that you have read about in this book – taking time to be still, enjoying the moment, being grateful, exercising – these are all tips that help your

---

[20] Jordon, R. (2015, June 30). *Stanford researchers find mental health prescription:* Nature. Standford: News. Retrieved from: http://news.stanford.edu/2015/06/30/hiking-mental-health-063015/

body, mind, and spirit to function at their optimal levels.

Researchers at the University of Minnesota have found that there are three benefits to being in Nature[21]:

- Nature has a healing effect. Apparently, whether we are in nature or simply viewing scenes of nature, it helps to reduce anger, fear, and stress while enhancing pleasant feelings within. Further the exposure to nature will help reduce blood pressure, heart rate, muscle tension, and the production of stress hormones.
- Nature has a soothing effect. Humans are genetically programmed to find trees, plants, water and other aspects of nature as relaxing and mesmerizing. So much so that nature scenes distract us from our pain and discomfort.
- Nature has a restorative effect. A study was conducted where 95% of the people interviewed reported having an

---

[21] Larson, J. and Kreitzer, M. (2016) How nature impacts our well being? *Taking Charge of Your Health & Wellbeing*. University of Minnesota. Retrieved from:
https://www.takingcharge.csh.umn.edu/enhance-your-wellbeing/environment/nature-and-us/how-does-nature-impact-our-wellbeing

improved mood after they spent time outside. Their moods changed from depressed, stressed, and anxious to more calm and balanced. Further, being in nature and viewing nature scenes also helped people to be more focused. It provided a respite for overactive minds.

Being in nature or viewing nature scenes has a positive impact on our nervous, endocrine, and immune systems. Staying physically healthy greatly impacts our spirit. When we are ill or stressed, it is more difficult – not impossible – to maintain a positive outlook and keep our spirits strong. Below are a few strategies to help you to be in nature:

> Get a plant. If you are anything like me then you may have difficulties keeping a plant alive. However, if you get a sturdy plant like a cactus or a plant with very thick leaves that holds water that should be helpful. Remember to talk to the plant – yes, speak to the plant. Some studies show that the carbon dioxide that we exhale when we speak helps the plant to grow. Also, a plant cannot speak back and so they are great listeners!

- Get a nature screen saver. We are often on our phones, on our computers, or on some electronic device. Having scenes of natures' beauty can help bring you to that calm and soothing place.
- Go for a walk. Schedule time for walks in nature. Get outside and get fresh air. If you live in a cold climate – bundle up – the fresh air will do you good!

Get Sleep & Drink Water

Get Sleep & Drink Water – These were also mentioned in Finesse Your Mind and the Finesse Your Body sections. The reason they are listed again is because of the importance of them. A healthy physical body and a sharp mind helps in fostering a positive and fulfilling spirit life. A key to a sharp mind and healthy body is to get effective rest and remain hydrated.

Your quality of sleep directly impacts your quality of wakefulness. Ensuring sufficient downtime is needed for your body to replenish and restore itself.

Drinking sufficient water is also very important. I know that the days where I do not drink water I'm not as alert, focused, or on point. I experience feelings of anxiousness and mild headaches that sometimes turn into migraines. Our bodies are made up of 60% water. It is imperative that we hydrate ourselves.

Below is a compilation of the previous tips related to sleep and hydration to ensure that you are getting enough sleep and water.

> ➤ Turn the computer/phone/electronic off at least an hour before you are going to go to sleep. The blue light from electronics can mess with what is called our circadian rhythm or our sleep/wake cycle. This cycle naturally tells our body when to sleep and when to be awake. Not a great thing to mess with!
> ➤ Avoid caffeine before going to bed. Caffeine will rob you of rest and keeps your heart rate up when it needs to relax to get into a good sleep rhythm.
> ➤ Turn off all lights and loud noises. You may think that you need music or other noises to soothe you to sleep, however, sound will stimulate the brain thus robbing the brain of its needed rest.
> ➤ Get your finances in order. Yep, you read correctly. Get your finances in order. One of the biggest robbers of sleep for people is the worry of their finances. Best advice I can give on this

one – you do not necessarily need to make more money but you do need to live within your means. Understand the role money plays and that it is used as a tool. Once you understand or gather knowledge about money, then you can decide whether your income needs to increase and then you can start to build wealth
- Remember the key is to drink eight glasses of water per day. Here is how:
- Have a glass of water/water bottle by your bedside table at night. When you wake up in the morning the first thing you do is drink it. Congrats, you've consumed one of the eight glasses before even getting out of bed!
- Have a glass of water before every meal and between every meal. Assuming you eat three times a day, now you have consumed six glasses right there.
- Have a glass before bed. There's number eight!

Laughter

Laughter – Have you ever had a good belly laugh? I mean the kind of belly laugh where you cannot breathe and tears are streaming down your face? Here is a stat for you. On average a child laughs 300-500 times per day whereas an adult laughs approximately 15 times per day. Just from observation – who seems happier – a child or an adult? Laughter helps you mentally and physically in that there are short term and long term effects. According to the Mayo Clinic, laughter induces physical and mental changes.[22] When you laugh, it will enhance the intake of oxygen-rich air which will stimulate your heart, lungs, and muscles while increasing the endorphins that are released by the brain. Laughter will also activate and relieve your stress response leaving you relaxed. What happens is that when you laugh deeply, your heart rate and blood pressure increase while cooling down your stress response. It soothes tension. On a long term basis, laughter can improve your immune system! Remember when we discussed how we tend to ruminate on negative thoughts? Well when we have negative thoughts they can manifest into chemical reactions that can impact the body by bringing more stress into the system and decreasing immunity. Positive thoughts, on the other hand, release neuropeptides that will help fight

---

[22] *Stress relief from laughter? It's no joke.* (2016, April 21). Mayo Clinic. Retrieved from: http://www.mayoclinic.org/healthy-lifestyle/stress-management/in-depth/stress-relief/art-20044456?pg=1

stress and potentially more serious illnesses. Laughter can also have the potential to relieve pain. When we laugh, it causes the body to produce its own natural painkillers. One of the most important aspects of laughter is that it can help to make difficult situations easier to cope with and helps us to connect more with others.

Have you heard of Laughter Yoga? Laughter Yoga has spread throughout North America. It allows laughter to spread contagiously through the group organically – no comedy or jokes. CNN has reported that Laughter Yoga has shown to improve health by decreasing stress, improving the immune system and increasing endorphins – the feel good chemicals our bodies produce that help with that euphoric feeling.

Taking care of your mind and body are helpful strategies to taking care of your spirit. It is truly a cycle where you need one to move successfully into the other. It's kind of like strawberries, chocolate sauce, and ice cream – all great on their own but oh so much better together! But seriously, it is a cycle that is needed for your success.

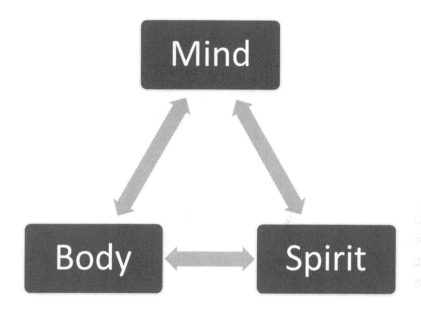

Change happens when the pain of staying the same is worse than the pain of making a change. Your mindset starts it all off. A positive mindset will allow you to make the necessary changes to your body as well as feed your spirit. It starts with your mind. Your spirit is your life – your exuberancy – your vitality. Feeding the spirit regularly feeds your mindset and helps you to develop strength and fortitude. Taking care of the house (body) where your mind and spirit reside is important. Do you want your Porsche and Mercedes to live in a shack or in a mansion? Your body is important. Good physical health helps make the implementation of the mind and spirit tips more effortless.

I read about a woman who was diagnosed with cancer and the doctors told her that the cancer was inoperable. The lady decided not to do radiation or chemotherapy. She took charge of her treatment and decided to heal herself. She went through her home and decided to get rid of everything even remotely negative – music, newspapers, magazines etc... She purchased movies – comedies – and invited her close family and friends over to watch with her. She laughed her way back to health. She did this for three months and when she went back to the doctor, they could not explain how the tumour shrunk to near nonexistence. Laughter helps cure the body, mind, and spirit.

Take a moment to make a list. On one side write down your ten favorite things to do. Then beside each of those items on your list, write down the feelings associated with it. No judgements!

My 10 Favorite Things To Do	My Feelings Associated with my 10 Favorite Things To Do

Now, you are going to repeat this process but this time, write down the ten things you ACTUALLY do most often in a day and the feelings associated with it.

The 10 things I ACTUALLY Do:	My Feelings Associated with the 10 Things I ACTUALLY Do

Are there any commonalities on your list?

Yes? No? (Circle one).

Which ones are similar on both lists?

1._____

2._____

3._____

4._____

5._____

6._____

7._____

8._____

9._____

10._____

The next instruction is simple but not necessarily easy. Do more of the things that bring you joy. Do less of the things that bring you down or make you sad. There are some things that we have to do whether we like it or not. However, there are ways of making those "have to" things more enjoyable – give yourself some reward at the end of that particular task – this is a type of cognitive behavioral therapy. You are conditioning your brain to feel positive feelings when doing a task that you do not particularly love.

This task is not as simple as you may think. It takes a bit of time and some meditation. Do not rush it. Take your time. Really analyze those feelings associated with the task. You may find that some of the "favorite" things that you like to do are actually not that good for you. For example, eating a bag of caramel popcorn in one sitting – not something I would suggest doing on a regular basis. Drinking alcohol in excess because it is a good escape – not a healthy choice. I am not condemning nor am I judging. I just want you to take stock of your actions. Change small, change often. That is how you will make significant change and impact in your life.

RECAP:

Ten tips:

1. Gratefulness
2. Reflection
3. Positive Affirmations
4. Replenish
5. Release
6. Prayer & Meditation
7. Family/Loved Ones
8. Nature

9. Get Sleep, Drink Water
10. Laughter

Which two can you start with?

_____
_____
_____
_____

I believe in changing small and changing often to create lasting change. I will be accountable to myself and to [insert your coach/accountability partner's name]

_____
__ with regards to my commitment to Finesse my Life – Spirit.

For each goal I will write down HOW I will implement the goal, WHEN I will implement the goal, WHAT my expectation and desired outcome is for the goal, and WHY this goal is important to me.

Remember, change small change often. Start with two and add as time goes on.

Starting on [insert date] _____ I will implement these two goals.

Record your success daily.

Finesse Your Life – Mind, Body, and Spirit

1._____
_____
_____
_____
_____
_____
_____
_____
_____
_____
_____
_____
_____
_____
_____

_____

Record your success daily.

2._____
_____
_____
_____
_____

Record your success daily.

As I begin to achieve my goals I will implement the other tips to add to my success!

3.

Record your success daily.

4.

Record your success daily.

5.

Record your success daily.

6.

Record your success daily.

7.
_____
_____
_____
_____
_____
_____
_____
_____
_____
_____
_____
_____
_____
_____
_____
_____
_____
_____
_____
_____
_____

Record your success daily.

8.

Record your success daily.

9.

Record your success daily.

10.

_____

Record your success daily.

So, do you have some work to do? I think it would be safe to bet – YES! You know how I know this? We all have work to do.

Self-improvement is a continual process.

Self-discovery is a continual process.

Self-love is a continual process.

We are always growing, changing, and rediscovering ourselves.

IT STARTS WITH BELIEF.

Out of all of the tips and strategies listed, setting a goal is one of the most important because it is going to make the difference between where you are and where you are going. Without goals we are just floating around and existing. Who the heck wants to do that? Share your greatness and your talent with the world the way only you can. Set a goal. Perhaps the first goal is setting aside/scheduling time to pray or meditate on a daily basis. Being still and feeling confident in what your next move will be. It may take discipline but the end result is happiness. Honestly, what can be better than that?

Remember, believe in yourself. You know in your heart that you have the ability to do great things. Allow your circumstances to push you forward. Fail forward as they say. You can do this. Believe it. Do it. Achieve it.

Believing in you now and always,

Jen

P.S. Go out there and Slay each and every day! You got this!
https://www.facebook.com/groups/FinesseYourLife/

About the Author

Jennifer Slay is a well-respected Women's Empowerment Coach, Counsellor, and the Creator of Finesse -skill in handling a highly sensitive situation – YOU. Finesse is a program that provides practical strategies to transform the everyday women into women of purpose, passion and worth. Jen's goal is to help women **be** happy, not simply feel happy. She is also the co-Founder of Pink Ink, a makeup and styling consulting firm that supports women in their journey to seeking increased confidence and results in both their professional and personal lives.

As a seasoned communicator whether it is speaking, writing or coaching, Jennifer has smart solutions to share. Her blog and social media posts are becoming extremely popular with her fans as she posts musings about life, style ideas and great ideas on how to better finesse your life. With a Master's in social work, Jennifer has had a seasoned career in helping the disadvantaged and with her focus now on developing healthy, wealthy and wise solutions for women who desire to change,

Jennifer has a busy and bright roster of clients. She specializes in working with professionals and community organizations to make a big impact and has been doing so for more than two decades.

Check out Jen at www.jenslay.com. Contact Jen at info@jenslay.com.

Made in the USA
Columbia, SC
08 August 2017